TIMEOUT

How to Achieve Peak Athletic Performance For
Elite Coaches, Athletes, and Teams Applying
The Principles of the Art of War

Coach M.D. Gross, MSM
Heather Williamson, Ph.D.

DEDICATION

This book is dedicated to the coach and player who understands what is needed to truly compete and NOT just receive the generic participation trophy.

TABLE OF CONTENTS

PRAISE FOR TIMEOUT

"Time-out" is a treasure trove of the fundamental secrets that champions have guarded for centuries and are often reluctant to share.

Playing for the Los Angeles Kings and competing against many future NHL Hall Of Fame players, such as Wayne Gretzky and Mark Messier, provided me insight into how world-class leaders and athletes did not just win; they dominated. For example, their Edmonton Oilers teams are considered dynasties, winning the Stanley Cup five out of seven years during my professional career.

In other words, a champion's continuous improvement tactics and strategies are based on a nonstop, tenacious analysis of strengths, weaknesses, opportunities, and threats. However, remember that even a skilled team with solid tactics and strategy will implode without trust.

How often have we seen topics featured in "Time Out," such as favoritism between coaches and players or even between players and players, deflate a team?

Coach Eric Germain
Former NHL Player - Los Angeles Kings
11 Year Professional Hockey Player

Coach Gross and Dr. Williamson created a well-organized guidebook for coaches in athletics, academics, and the corporate world to motivate and develop high-performing individuals. "Time Out" is easy to read and clutter-free, taking the best allegorical elements of sports-related cinema and distilling it to its essence to provide leaders with an essential tool for their toolkit."

Professional Strategist
Dr. Matthew Steele
Alumni - Virginia Commonwealth University

Using creative visual examples, "Time Out" successfully introduces and reinforces The Art of War's critical principles, including the importance of dropping our egos. How often have leaders failed to prepare or adapt compared to their competition?

As a former dual-sport collegiate athlete, a professional player for a decade, and a current coach, both manuscripts have timeless, well-presented lessons. Specifically, even if you dominate at your current level, your competition will aggressively plan and adjust their plans to achieve victory.

Finally, growing up as the son of a collegiate coach, "Time Out" reinforced the fundamental lessons for victory my father taught me, which are thousands of years old and still relevant to victory.

Coach Bruce MacDonald
Philadelphia Flyers Draft Pick
D1 Hockey Player- University of New Hampshire
D1 Lacrosse Player - University of New Hampshire
Toledo Storm East Coast Hockey League Champion

"TIMEOUT"

"TIMEOUT" is the first strategic word many coaches and athletes hear in their early athletic competitions. Starting in our homes, neighborhoods, schoolyards, and first teams, we naturally discover that we physically need an informal or formal stoppage in play. While our endurance levels may vary, we eventually realize that no one is immune to fatigue or injury. Not you and not me. You will even see this when comparing a novice to a professional competitor. It's important to note that while every human body is different, coaches and athletes should always remember that they are not unbreakable machines.

Comparing a human to an unbreakable machine may sound extreme, but this is essential since the mythical indestructible machine has never been invented. Yet, coaches still forget this important fact in their desire to win. Furthermore, since we are not machines, we must consider timeouts, a strategic tactic that can be used to regroup and strategize. Stoppages in competition from a tactical, technical, and psychological perspective must be well-thought-out.

As you can see, the concept of a timeout can become complicated. You may even be wondering if there is a book or blueprint that can help you navigate strategy, tactics, and technical and psychological challenges. The good news is that there are, and you may have already been exposed to, many of its principles. For example, if you have ever heard the saying that you should attack a person or team's weaknesses and avoid their strengths, you may be familiar with an ancient manuscript that many have referenced but want to keep private.

This manuscript, of course, is *The Art of War*. Do a quick internet search of this timeless classic's many books, articles, and interpretations, and you may realize you know more about its strategic lessons than you thought. As a visual example of our main points, we have included examples from sports movie scenes you may have watched, or we suggest rewatching from a new perspective. To clear up any potential criticism, we know that many of these movies, while based on real-life events, may have been altered and thus impacted historical accuracy. Because movie makers may have taken "artistic liberties" with real-life stories or events, it is always suggested to research further, but that is not the purpose of this book.

This book aims to help introduce, simplify, and provide insights into proven winning concepts that are just as relevant today as they were over 2,500 years ago. *The Art of War* may initially seem complex to many coaches and players; thus, we provide a supplemental athletic handbook for those teams seeking continuous improvement. While the definition of an "elite" coach, athlete, or team may sometimes seem subjective, when we use the word "elite," we are targeting objective goals for pro, college, and varsity competitors, which should always include continuous improvement. Furthermore, since it is impossible to include every topic or perspective, we will keep it simple and stick to the main points for Vol. 1. Before we start, remember that legendary winning coaches and players may have used *The Art of War* way before you have and are often secretive.

In addition to using *The Art of War* as a framework for this book, we also use *Magnetic Trust*. *Magnetic Trust*, written by Dr. Heather Williamson, the co-author of this book, shares the importance of building trust between your players, staff, and schools to achieve success. As a coach, if you don't have the trust of your team, they will not follow you to victory. Identifying what needs to be done to build trust and implementing the plan will lead you down the path of victory that every coach and team desires.

Good news is...You have already taken the first step in beating your competition in advance at their own game, which is calling… **TIMEOUT.**

CHAPTER 1

ATHLETIC ART OF LAYING PLANS

Athletic Art of Laying Plans

> **"***Success is won by those who believe in winning and then prepare for that moment. Many want to win, but how many prepare? That is the big difference. A sound value system held water then, holds water today, and will hold water in the future.***"**
>
> – **Herb Brooks,**
> Hockey Hall of Fame Coach

Have you ever seen an athlete, coach, or player win a competition due to their elite ability to plan yet remain flexible?

While many chapters of *The Art of War* may be read out of sequence, it is suggested that elite coaches and athletes always remember two cornerstone lessons for success that are powerfully stated in the above quote. Herb Brooks, who engineered what many sports historians have labeled as one of the greatest upsets of all sports, was the 1980 U.S. Olympic Gold Winning hockey team coach who epitomizes why you always start with the same end state. Successful professional, collegiate, and varsity competitors understand that their end state is winning. However, more is needed to believe in winning at an elite level. You must prepare and plan to succeed.

Picture this: For an excellent visual example of these two concepts, viewers should watch or rewatch a specific scene from the movie *Miracle*. In this 2004 classic, Herb Brooks, played by Kurt Russell is seen early in the film sitting in a waiting room where he is about to interview for the head coach role for the U.S. Olympic team in 1979. As he sits in the waiting room, he is meticulous in planning, and it is witnessed immediately as he is diagraming on his tactics board. Remember, he has yet to be hired for the job but he's acting as though he has already accepted the position.

While interviewing for the job, he explained to the committee that the team would require significant improvement changes. For example, before the Olympic games, he wanted to increase more brutal team competitions to improve the player's skills, conditioning, speed, and team chemistry. From a budgetary perspective alone, he is already facing opposition to his plan since this will be costly. Simply put, more games automatically require more travel costs and equipment. However, when he reveals his plans to change the U.S. teams' style of play to new methods, he is nearly booted out of the room.

Without playing a movie spoiler, the story of the 1980 Olympic hockey team and Herb Brooks as head coach is vital for several reasons. The first and most important is that Coach Brooks had a plan! Coach Brooks continues to explain his plan, which sounds impossible to the board, since he has goals of not only winning a medal, but also beating the Russian team, which many consider one of the best Olympic teams ever.

As seen in the movie *Miracle*, *The Art of War* references winning in advance, which means it is vital that you plan. While there may be cases where you can beat your competition by not planning when you face adversity, especially when competing on an elite level (pro, college, varsity), a lack of a plan will often result in defeat. It would be best to prepare for the best and worst-case scenarios when facing a rival.

TIMEOUT
- Additional Important Planning Factors to Consider within The Art of War:

- Identify your coaches, players, and schools' strengths, weaknesses, opportunities, and threats before planning your game strategy.

- Remain flexible when preparing short or long-term goals that may need to be revised.

- Make planning a collaborative effort; coaches and players should work together as this creates a sense of ownership.

- Never allow egos to impede your goal, which is consistently winning.

- Keep all plans secretive to your opponents and utilize deception.

Regardless of your individual or team plan, remember that even the best plans go awry if the coaches and players are not united. Remember that your plans will eventually fail if you lack player trust.

Suggested Continuous Improvement Process or Tool

A great tool to help you and your team plan is by performing a SWOT analysis. SWOT analysis will allow you to identify, and plan based on strengths, weaknesses, opportunities, and threats. See Chapter 15 to learn how you may implement a SWOT analysis into your planning tactics and strategy.

❧ How Planning Contributes To Building Trust

Why do some teams seem to have that undeniable chemistry where everyone is in sync?

You know what I mean...

The players read one another, the coach reads the players, and the players read the coach anticipating what each other will say and do simply through their non-verbal's. Well, I can guarantee it wasn't because of luck! The team's chemistry results from intentional planning in the coaching process and relationship. This was exemplified perfectly in the movie, *Miracle*. Coach Brooks had a plan to create the best hockey team in the U.S.A. The plan included playing hockey teams better than his, longer practices, specific drills to improve stamina, and much more; Coach Brooks tells his new team that if they give 99%, it will make his job very, very easy. Coach Brooks also states that he will be their coach; he won't be their friend. By stating this, Coach Brooks sets the stage for his plan on making them a great team and defining what his role will be in the process. Trust develops when players understand what is expected of them from the moment they join the team until the last game of the season.

Trust is the glue that holds relationships together. Athletes need to trust their coaches and coaches need to trust their athletes. When mutual trust exists, it becomes magnetic! But trust doesn't happen automatically... there is a lot of thought and planning that goes into developing the relationship. As a coach, it's crucial to not only think about the current season but also two to three seasons out. Identify who is currently on the team, who can play two roles, in case a player gets hurt. What position gaps do I have if a player leaves at the end of the season? What coach or athletic director is looking to move up the athletic ladder? How is this going to impact the team and organization?

The same planning is required when you see bottlenecks such as having your mind set on a player or play. The establishment of processes is a must to achieve success. When processes are established, you have a resource to refer to as situations or questions arise. Always remember that sometimes processes need to be changed depending on the situation. That's OK. Just don't be too stuck in your conviction that you ignore it.

Players see when a tactic or team member isn't working, and the coach lets it slide. Your players trust you to not let this happen. You might be thinking… is having the trust of my players really that important? They should just do what I tell them to do. Right? Well, in an ideal world, that might be true, but the TRUST of your players is a requirement if you want a high-performing sports team.

As a coach, your players trust that you have planned out everything to the smallest detail related to winning a game. This includes knowing the opposing coach and how they lead, understanding the strengths and weaknesses of their players and the competing team, and ensuring that each player is in a position that aligns with their strengths.

In addition, your players trust you to provide guidance and expertise in one-on-one coaching for skill development and education, so they become the best athletes for your team. Your players trust you to know them so well that they will excel and succeed. All of this and more takes time and planning.

So, take the time to plan how you will win. What needs to happen to make that plan work? Remember that having your athlete's trust in you as their coach is part of the plan. That means from the minute you walk into your office to being on the field, building trust should be part of the plan.

As a coach, you can get your players to trust that you are planning effectively by-

1) **Communicating that planning for anything is a step-by-step process.** Planning includes considering what you know and what you don't know.

2) **Work with your players on action plans and believe in their success.**

3) **When planning,** solicit feedback from your players to identify concerns or perceived lack of skill or knowledge so you can quickly correct them.

Chapter 2

ATHLETIC ART OF WAGING WAR COMPETITION

Athletic Art of Waging War Competition

"I believe that a team is a group of people with one vision with one objective and by God one heartbeat!"

– Herman Boone,
Head Coach of The Titans

Have you ever seen an athlete, coach, or player win a competition due to their ability to be resilient?

As we have read in the first chapter, planning is vital. However, in Chapter 2, we must immediately remember that even the greatest plans are worthless if they cannot be executed. In addition, it is no secret amongst elite coaches and athletes that even the best plans are unpredictable. While there are many controllable scenarios within the competition, we must know there will always be uncontrollable situations that no one could have predicted. While the fans may enjoy the volitivity of competition, elite coaches and athletes who have read *The Art of War* know that the ability to maintain their solidarity during uncertain times is a tactical advantage.

Picture this: for a visual example of how we adapt and still execute when things do not go as planned, we can use a scene from *Remember The Titans* where Coach Boone, played by (Denzel Washington) faces an unexpected injury. In this situation, his quarterback, who appears to be irreplaceable, suffers an injury at the worst time. However, Boone has prepared for the unexpected and knows they must be flexible and adjust if they want to win. Most viewers may see a coach replacing his starter with another capable quarterback ready to execute. However, elite coaches and athletes know that the valid reason they could not miss a beat against their rivals was based on team cohesion.

Great coaches and athletes understand that they will face adversity when trying to achieve their goals. Furthermore, during competition, there are infinite opinions on adjusting your execution when trouble strikes. However, successful teams must be unified in their vision and objectives, even if they may disagree. Yet sharing the same heartbeat shows you are in sync with each other and, as a result, are often much more successful than a team divided. This is why the above quote by the real Coach Herman Boone is essential, even if it was not utilized in this movie scene.

TIMEOUT

- Additional Important Planning Factors to Consider within The Art of War:

- We must see even our friends as rivals when competing in practice. Sharpen each other.

- Never forget that a team winning should be prioritized over individual accomplishments.

- Practices should be more exhausting than games, and our goal is to end games quickly.

- Don't motivate your competition before, during, or after based on your speech or actions.

- Do not wait to make tactical or technical adjustments as needed during competition. (Example: switching players or formations, etc.)

Suggested Continuous Improvement Process or Tool

A great tool to help you and your team plan is designing a "roles and responsibilities matrix". Understanding, establishing and practicing these factors in advance will provide you an advantage over your competition. See Chapter 15 to learn how you may implement a roles and responsibilities matrix into your planning tactics and strategy.

♠ How Competence Builds Trust

Would you trust your coach if you believe they lacked the skills or knowledge to lead a winning team?

When competing in a game, the athlete and coach expect that 'practice' is over and 'performance' is occurring. 'Performing' results from many hours of 'practice' to learn the skills so they are ingrained into your muscle memory. Once the skills are part of your muscle memory, they become a habit that does not require thought. The action is automatic.

But how does an athlete or coach exhibit the competence needed to create trust? A coach's competence is exhibited when they know their team so well that when a tactic is necessary during a play, they know immediately who can accomplish it and who can't. I refer to this approach as vertical. Competence also includes knowledge of the opposing team and coach and being open to ideas or tactics used in the past. Coaches have their favorite plays and will use them until they are ineffective. Competent coaches are consistently studying their competition to see what tactics and strategies are being used so they can develop a proactive defense or offense. I refer to this as a horizontal approach to competence.

When a coach or player is reactive, this is a sign that they lack competence.

Athletes must learn to trust in their abilities so the skills they have been practicing becomes a normal and natural behavior, especially on game day. Or more simply put... a habit. Likewise, the coach learns to trust in their players, through the many hours of practice, that they have the skills and competence to perform the strategies to win the game.

Having the skills is important, we also know that mindset plays a huge role in the success and failure of any competition. When Coach Boone says, "I'm a winner. I'm going to win." He is modeling the practice of saying affirmations. In his mind, Coach Boone was already committed to winning the competition. Coach Boone can visualize the win in his head and can feel the emotional excitement from it as well. Once visualized, the big job is to convey this image and feeling so his team also feels and believes it. That means getting his athletes to trust and believe they are winners. Because this is so important, I won't leave you hanging.

As a coach, you can get your players to trust in themselves by-

1) Focusing on inquiry, curiosity, and questioning one another on why a play or decision was made.

2) Communicating both positive and corrective feedback to reinforce the desired skills needed to win.

3) Encouraging your players to develop their own affirmations, so they are owned and believed.

CHAPTER 3

ATHLETIC ART OF ATTACK BY STRATEGY

The Art of Strategy

"It began, really, with an innocent question: how did one of the poorest teams in baseball, the Oakland Athletics, win so many games."

Michael Lewis,
Author of Moneyball: THE ART OF WINNING AN UNFAIR GAME

Have you ever seen an athlete, coach, or player win a competition due to their elite ability to change their strategy based on their strengths?

As we transition from planning and execution during competitions, we must remember one of the essential lessons introduced in *The Art of War*: everything elite coaches and athletes do should be based on deception and surprise when competing. This means that even if you have yet to make plans to change your plans or execution, your opponents should never know your intentions. Keep them guessing and shock them, if you want to win.

Picture this: In the movie *Moneyball*, The Oakland A's general manager, Billy Beane (played by Brad Pitt), is facing improbable odds of winning games against superior rivals. Using the third chapter from *The Art of War* intentionally or unintentionally, Beane surprised even his closest advisors with an audacious strategy.

In one scene, Billy Beane is in a room full of Athletics scouts and the organization's brain trust. They are trying to figure out how to replace the three players they lost to teams with more money who can ultimately buy the best players from cash-strapped organizations, such as their own. Knowing that his current strategy is not working, he debuts his concept of ignoring the financial hardships and focusing on statistical analytics that had been ignored in the past. Ultimately, he assembled a team of less desirable players who nevertheless fit into the Athletics' budget and new statistical perspective. Specifically, the Boston Red Sox and New York Yankees pursued players who were considered the best players in the game from weaker, financially limited organizations.

Underdogs often win because their competitors are unaware of their tactics, strategies, and execution ability. Their deception or surprise may be that they say they are making changes yet are steadfast in their game plans and lure others into confusion. Ultimately, you want to be unpredictable to get an advantage over opponents.

> # TIMEOUT
> ## - Important Strategy Factors to Consider within the Art of Strategy:

- Everything in athletics at an elite level is based on strategy.

- Strategy alone will not win your games, but its absence will contribute to defeats.

- The ultimate strategy in *The Art of War* is knowing when to attack and defend.

- Prepare your strategy not only for superior opponents but also for inferior ones.

- Avoid falling into the trap of groupthink when developing strategies; everybody doesn't always agree with a plan.

Suggested Continuous Improvement Process or Tool

Implementing process mapping is a great tool to help you and your team improve. Having a visual map of where you have been, currently are, and plan to be is often a tactic only elite teams follow but are unwilling to share. See Chapter 15 to learn how you may implement process mapping into your tactics and strategies.

♠ How Innovation Leads To Trust

As a coach or administrator, how open are you to trying outside-the-box innovative tactics?

Having a strategy also includes ensuring that the coach and player clearly understand how their roles impact the team. The role athletes play is determined by their positions. For instance, I remember in 2011 watching my alma-mater, Virginia Commonwealth University, play in the Final Four of the NCAA Tournament against Butler University. Each basketball player knew their role; such as point guard, shooting guard or center, and focused on the behaviors needed to get a basket. For instance, the point guard's role is to dribble the basketball down the court. The center often stands near the goal, waiting to get a rebound and make a basket. Every basketball coach knows this. The question begs...how can you make this innovative?

Imagine if you had five players on the court, and each player went full speed down the court in an uncontrolled free-for-all, trying to get the ball down and score. The result is exciting but also can lead to CHAOS!!! Players and fans may love this strategy of an all-out offensive attack. But an innovative strategy Coach Shaka Smart implemented during his coaching tenure at Virginia Commonwealth University, was completely the opposite. He based his teams' systems on a high-pressure defense where you can trap and control your opponent's actions on both sides of the courts, regain possession, and counterattack immediately. He called his HAVOC.

Coach Smart trained his team by running drills constantly. Players' stamina was built to ensure their ability to last through a game without pooping out in the second half. A consistent fast-paced approach was innovative and many other basketball coaches soon used the same tactic when they found their players were pooping out during the second half.

Coach Smart didn't follow the path that had always been followed. Coach Smart thought outside the box by looking at what could be done differently to gain an advantage against another team. Avoiding groupthink is so important because people want to follow the norms of conformity to achieve a cohesive team. However, sometimes, you just mix it up and go against the established norms. Don't be anxious or scared because of what the news media will say or the lack of clicks you get on social media. If you give the power to the press, innovation will always be a struggle.

As a coach, you can learn to be innovative by-

1) **Involve others.** Involving others means including others in the development of ideas. Remember your team is made up of many players with diverse experiences. Use this to brainstorm new tactics or strategies.

2) **Focus on the problem.** Dig deep and understand the issue preventing you from achieving your goals. Once you identify an innovative strategy, test it against your assumptions. Don't let fear hold you back.

3) **Continually improve with the focus on being objective.** Follow the 3 R's by reviewing, revising, and releasing/implementing the tactic.

CHAPTER 4

ATHLETIC ART OF TACTICAL DISPOSITIONS

The Art of Tactical Dispositions

After the shooting ended, Hackman gave each actor who portrayed Hickory players a plaque. Valainis' reads: "I'll make it."

Maris Valainis,
who played Jimmy Chitwood in Hoosiers

Have you ever seen an athlete, coach, or player win a competition due to their elite ability to use tactics based on their positioning?

Building on our early planning, execution, and strategic concepts, we transition into tactics during Chapter 4. As a quick refresher, remember that your tactics are how you plan to achieve your strategy. With that in mind, athletic tactics often focus on how you set up formations, arrange your teams, and ultimately move. To an outsider, when their teams are winning, they may need to comprehend how much thought and practice is placed into positioning before a competition. However, a successful coach or athlete will often rehearse their movements not only on a physical level but also psychologically.

Picture this: A visual example of a team that has successfully mastered its movements well in advance can be seen in the movie *Hoosiers.* In one of the most pivotal scenes in the film Coach Norman Dale (Hackman's role) has his underdog team on the verge of winning a state championship. Ironically, he calls a timeout late in the game to make tactical adjustments and set up for a final play. During the timeout, Coach Dale explains that the other team will expect their best player (Jimmy Chitwood) to take the shot, so he sets up a formation to get it to another teammate instead. As the timeout is about to expire and Coach Dale sends the team back in to execute his tactics, he senses a severe lack of confidence in his team. When Coach Dale asks them what is wrong, they all look at each other, afraid to express their thoughts, yet Jimmy Chitwood says, "I'll make it." As a result, the coach changed his tactics, and they won the game.

This may seem unreal, with the players questioning the coach's tactics and overruling him in the huddle. But, if you were to see the entire movie based on a true story, you would understand that the coach was in control the whole time. He would only have asked for their feedback if he were interested in his team's thinking. This leads to an essential point on individual or team movements. It is always good to drop your egos and seek outside feedback. Tactics cannot be ego-driven because getting buy-in from the team and establishing trust is challenging during preparation. Yet imagine how important it is to get accurate feedback in real-time situations during games if confidence is lacking, but your communication could be better. While the coach is the final decision-maker regarding how team tactics will be chosen and executed, collaborating is vital to adjust quickly when needed.

T I M E O U T

- Important Tactical Factors to Consider within the Art of Tactical Dispositions:

- Never neglect a strong defense, even in a strong attacking position.

- Consistently include feints within your tactics.

- Understand the differences between your risks and opportunities.

- Momentum is an intangible that must constantly be monitored.

- Forecast and monitor your opponent's tactical decisions.

Suggested Continuous Improvement Process or Tool

Utilizing surveys is a great tool to help you and your team improve. Obtaining honest feedback and tracking your progress are vital steps to monitor progress. See Chapter 15 to learn how you may implement surveys into your tactics and strategies.

✒ How Personal Accountability and Leading From The Front Builds Trust in Your Team

As a coach, do you own your mistakes or play the blame game?

As a coach, you must have the answers and tactics to win a game. This is because you have done your homework. You have studied the opposing team's plays and analyzed their players. You know what their coach's next move will be. You also know the strengths and weaknesses of the opposing team's players. Based on this information, you OWN the tactics to use in the game to ensure a win.

But what happens when your player has another tactic?

Do you stick with your tactic and gut? Or trust in your player to follow through on their tactic that is based on the success of past performance? It's a tough decision.

The questions I have for you are... Do you trust your player? Do you trust in yourself?

If the answer is YES, then the decision is much easier. If the answer is NO, you need to ask yourself WHY and WHAT you have not done as a coach to have answered YES.

Could it be that you think you have a better strategy or tactic? Could the player be egotistical and want to play, not thinking that their streak has gone "cold"? Or does the player need more experience or information to decide on the tactic?

Whatever your answer, the bottom line is that you don't TRUST your player. This lack of trust is all on you.

Yes, there is a transparent chain of command. You want your players to take ownership of the play and their position. However, whether the play is successful or not, YOU authorized the play. Now you must OWN it. I'll also add here that you should never take ownership of the wins as a coach. Wins should be given to the team. Your coaching led to the win, but you will look like a major jerk if you take ownership of the wins while passing the failures onto the team.

As a coach, you can learn to OWN your actions by-

1) **Lead by example.** If a play doesn't go as planned show your team that you own the failure and are looking for ways to achieve success.

2) **Be bold and call out a player when needed, but privately and not publicly.** Your team is watching how you handle challenges.

3) **Accept responsibility for losses;** don't play the blame game.

CHAPTER 5

ATHLETIC ART OF ENERGY

The Art Of Energy

"Attitude is more important than aptitude. I can build a football team with guys that have somewhat limited ability but a great attitude."

Jack Lengyel,

Former Head Football coach on which the film We Are Marshall is based

------

Have you ever seen an athlete, coach, or player win a competition due to their elite motivation ability?

Is it possible to plan, execute, implement, have a great game plan, and still be continually beaten by a team that is stronger or faster than your own? If you have been involved in athletics for any period and have been defeated by a weaker team, you know the answer is always yes. So many factors may contribute to a loss or a win, but we cannot underestimate how powerful a coach, athlete, or team's attitude can play in which side of the scoreboard you end up on when the whistle or horn blows.

While *The Art of War* may not focus specifically on attitudes within the book, imagine how it may affect competition. Scientific factors such as energy, momentum, force, and even speed can be represented as data. However, how do you measure, motivate, and seek continuous improvement, even when facing adversity? Picture this: In the movie, *We Are Marshall* when the energetic head coach Jack Lengyel, portrayed by an energetic Matthew McConaughey puts his team in a position to pull off an upset in the final seconds of a game. Matthew McConaughey turns to his assistant and powerfully demonstrates how powerful an attitude plays in energy.

Even in such a stressful time, he remains optimistic and smiles, instilling confidence in telling his assistant coach to finish the game with a final play decision. Without hesitation, in a matter of seconds, the energy and positive attitude move from the head coach to the assistant coach to the player tasked with executing the play. In a predictable Hollywood ending, everything works out perfectly. However, a point many non-coaches and athletes may have yet to notice is how vital the flashback montage is during the final play.

During the flashback montage, the adversity the Marshall team needed to overcome and win a game is not your standard storyline. For example, Marshall lost a large portion of their football program in a horrific plane crash. As a result, this tragedy was so severe to the University and its community that it was in jeopardy of being cut indefinitely. However, in seconds, you are reminded that the reason the team and community are victorious on and off the field goes beyond a rah-rah speech from a coach. The attitudes of all those involved affected the team's momentum and, arguably, their speed and force. Both teams were probably exhausted later in this game but pay attention to who had the energy. You may be surprised...

TIMEOUT

- Important Tactical Factors to Consider within the Art of Energy:

- Successful teams exhibit fast and positive energy and communication from all levels.

- Winning teams know how to rapidly get the right people in the correct positions at the right time.

- Never forget that there are two ways to attack: indirect and direct.

- Mislead your opponents to your actual energy levels.

- Know when to attack, defend, and rest.

Suggested Continuous Improvement Process or Tool

A great tool to help motivate you and your team is benchmarking. Benchmarking will allow you to monitor your energy levels and morale. See Chapter 15 to learn how you may implement benchmarking into your tactics and strategy.

☙ The Power of Authenticity and How It Influences Trust

Have you had a situation where a player(s) disrespected you or refused to follow your direction?

Being authentic as a leader and coach is so important. It is one of the most important characteristics a leader and coach should possess. Authenticity comes from being self-aware and knowing who you are as a person. An authentic coach allows his players and assistant coaches to truly know who he is. An authentic coach also knows what type of team is needed for a winning season. If building leaders on and off the field or court is essential to you, then do it. Bottom line, show your love for the sport!

A coach that is authentic shows when they are excited as well as frustrated. If you are ramped up at a game, show it. Don't be fake and act like you do not care. Suppose one of your players made a fantastic play, praise that player for a successful play. Being authentic also means you communicate with a player when they screw up. Don't be afraid to show your emotions. However, as a leader and coach you should never show fear.

When your players see fear, they will lack confidence and trust in you, and experience fear themselves. So, show appropriate emotions, but be careful not to show them when panicking or fearing. Demonstrate that you are in control of the situation and have a plan. If you are stuck because a play did not go as planned (and they will), ask your assistant coach for help. Utilize your coaching staff to help problem-solve.

I will be honest here... one of my biggest pet peeves is when a coach isn't truthful with a player. For example, respectfully tell the player if you have zero intentions of putting a player into a game, as well as your reasoning why, based on your current perspective. You are being deceptive when you are not forthright about what may be needed for improvement and increased playing time. Perhaps, this year it is all about skill development, so the player is ready next year. This is also true for a player who has started the whole season and is suddenly sitting on the bench without any explanation. A player will lose motivation and give up, if a coach consistently strings the player along and does not help them achieve their goals. A coach's lack of authenticity may result in not having a potential great player the following year.

Just imagine you have two athletes... one athlete is always happy, energetic, motivated, and confident in their ability to succeed. The other athlete is always negative, defeated, and lacks energy. As a coach, which athlete would you want on your team for the big game?

Exactly. The athlete that has a positive attitude and is disciplined to put forth the required effort to train and perform. The athlete listens and learns from the coach to develop their skills and knowledge further. The athlete is aggressive on the field and anticipating the opponent's next move.

As a coach, you can learn to be authentic by-

1) **Becoming self-aware and knowing who you are as a person.** Do not allow others to tell you what you want if it does not align with your values and beliefs.

2) **Know your strengths and weaknesses.** who possess attributes that you may be missing or lacking in.

3) **Exhibit commitment and passion.** Share your passion and drive to be the best for the sport.

ATHLETIC ART OF WEAK AND STRONG POINTS

The Art Of Weak and Strong Points

"I'd rather be with the strongest than the weakest...."

Brian Clough,
Renowned Strategic and Tactical Manager

Have you ever seen an athlete, coach, or player win a competition due to their ability to identify strengths, weaknesses, opportunities, and threats?

As previously mentioned, *The Art of War* does not necessarily need to be read, interpreted, or implemented in an exact chronological process. Yes, an argument can be made that planning must always be done first to win. However, situations may change so quickly in a competition that your opposition's failure to plan successfully may present you with advantages that need immediate action. Of course, quick changes do not mean planning is unnecessary; you must be agile to deal with many unexpected competitive advantages and disadvantages.

Rather than using the advantages and disadvantages terminology, you may have heard them referred to in athletics as strengths and weaknesses. Furthermore, you may have heard of common phrases teams say, such as "We need to know our strengths and weaknesses." Or "We need to know the weaknesses and strengths of our opponents." However, the elite coach understands that while both comments are essential, they are only helpful if they can be used to exploit your competition.

Picture this: In *The Damned United* when legendary professional soccer coach Brian Clough (Derby County) prepares to compete with a superior competitor, Leeds United. As Clough runs a pregame practice with his assistant, he is aware of the strengths and weaknesses of his team. Yet, Clough also has a false sense of confidence in believing that he knows the Leeds coach so well that he ignores a significant detail that evolved during the game. That is his opponent is at a different level, not only skill wise but is able to control the game out of pure physical dominance and intimidation. Clough makes a crucial error early in his career, perhaps due to overconfidence or lack of agility, to attack his opponent's strengths, ultimately leading to a defeat.

T I M E O U T
- Important Tactical Factors to Consider within the Art of Weak and Strong Points:

- Always conceal your strengths and weaknesses outside of your organization.

- Know your opponent's technical and tactical skills well, but don't forget how they may unexpectedly change based on different scenarios, such as weather, terrain, or environments.

- Avoid becoming predictable; surprise is often the catalyst when momentum shifts during competition.

- Never telegraph your intentions, either visually or on an audible level.

- Be careful of deceptive traps, but when your opponent is tired, this is often the best time to be agile and attack. Remember, you may also fake tiredness to present a weakness.

Suggested Continuous Improvement Process or Tool

A great tool to help you avoid groupthink and complacency is brainstorming. Brainstorming not only allows you to generate a lot of new ideas in a short period but also keeps your opponent guessing on your next steps. See Chapter 15 to learn how you may implement brainstorming into your tactics and strategy.

♣ How Great Communication Skills Builds Trust

How are your communication skills on a scale from 1- bad to 10- exceptional?

If you rate yourself a perfect 10, you may need to read this chapter immediately since it is possible you are suffering from overconfidence and missing a major blind spot for improvement. Bottomline, often narcissistic self-views on communication lead to the downfall of many great coaches. If you are rating yourself lower than a 10, congratulations you understand there are always additional opportunities for improvement in how you communicate with your team and staff.

Clear communication is critical for success. Clear communication means that you explain ideas in a concise and straightforward message so that it is understood. Clear messages include goal expectations, feedback on player performance, and reiterating messages identified as necessary.

How is your message understood?

Clear communication involves having excellent listening skills. Utilizing active listening skills is critical. For example, when you give tactical or drill strategies to your players, ensure you confirm their understanding. Coaches should explain the WHY behind decisions, so staff and players understand the reasoning. Coaches can confirm understanding by asking players/staff to repeat what was just communicated and why it is essential to know.

An effective coach will ask questions and encourage players to ask questions. Understanding how your players think will help you strategize game plays. Coaches that focus on building staff and player trust don't play psychological games such as hyping up a player or parent. Instead, they communicate expectations and focus on a team agenda.

Communication is about more than just the words that are spoken. Communication is also shared through non-verbal actions taken and tone of voice. Albert Mehrabian, a researcher of body language studied face to face communication and found over ninety-three percent of communication is done through nonverbals. Nonverbal cues include rolling of the eyes, huffing and puffing, throwing up the hands in frustration, clapping after a great play, and much more. Only seven percent of the words spoken make up what is being communicated. When communicating, make sure that your nonverbals (55%), tone of voice (38%), and words (7%) are in alignment to ensure that your message is received and interpreted the way you intended. If your message is not aligned, it will be muddled and confusing.

Most communication is done through nonverbals and will benefit you to be mindful of their cues. Recognition of nonverbals is extremely important when assessing player and staff engagement.

- If your player is gazing across the court or field and not paying attention to what you are communicating, the player is disengaged.

- If your player is talking with a fellow player and not listening to what you are saying, the player(s) are not engaged.

- If your player or staff member is consistently late to practice or team meetings, they are disengaged.

Acknowledging when this occurs and asking why it is happening is vital to gain understanding. Once a coach understands why a player or staff member behaves in a certain way, questioning and action to change it can happen. When a coach is intentional about communicating and listening, trust will develop.

As a coach, you can learn to be a better communicator by-

1) **Practicing active listening skills.**

2) **Being more intentional in reading nonverbal behaviors.**

3) **Communicate clear expectations.** Ensure your nonverbals, tone of voice, and words are aligned.

CHAPTER 7

ATHLETIC ART OF MANEUVERING

The Art of Art of Maneuvering

"Find out what the other team wants to do. Then take it away from them."

George Halas,
NFL Hall Of Fame Coach

Have you ever seen an athlete, coach, or player win a competition due to their elite ability to outmaneuver others?

One key concept that may appear simple on the surface yet is complex in *The Art of War* is based on how coaches and athletes react to opportunities. As mentioned in our previous chapter on weak and strong points, you must remain agile and know when to attack when a weakness is present. Meaning you need to maneuver to win and cannot remain stagnant. Yes, an argument can be made for staying stationary when winning in some situations to run out a clock, tire your opponents, etc. However, the reality is that in most sports now, there are rules in place to prevent this from occurring since it may not be spectator-friendly.

Spectators want movement, not a deadlock of two competitors standing still for strategic or tactical advantages. This is why a shot clock was introduced in basketball, and delay of game penalties were added to most sports. Even Major League Baseball, considered one of the most traditional sports, implemented a pitch clock. But let's look at it beyond the spectator's perspective; the quote above from George Halas makes sense.

Picture this: In a tense scene from the movie *Brian's Song* (original or remake) when Coach Halas is talking to his two halfbacks. His eventual Hall of Fame running back, Gayle Sayers, returns to his starting role after a significant injury. Anxiety and tension are already in the air for several reasons. First, is Sayers ready, and is the time right for this move? Also, who will back him up if he needs to be replaced again? Previously, Sayers's best friend Brian Piccolo had done a great job, and even their competitors would expect this to be the coach's next move. However, Halas explains that will not be the case since another rookie player will now be his number two halfback.

Not only would this surprise his opponents, but as you can see in the scene, it surprises both Sayers and Piccolo who both appear disgruntled. On the surface, the coach is just making a lineup change to bolster his team with a younger, perhaps quicker backup to Sayers. However, it is also revealed that Halas is changing Piccolo's position from halfback to fullback to get both players on the field simultaneously. In retrospect, this concept has been introduced; getting the best players into the best positions at the correct times maximizes a team's performance. But it also shows that Halas knew his players beyond their skills. Outside of chalkboard strategies and tactics, he considered the psychological aspects of his decisions to increase performance and build trust. Meaning, beyond physical maneuvering, he also regarded it as a psychological opportunity. Sayers will return to the game with a healthy yet inexperienced halfback, but his best friend can protect him, and his backup, in the same backfield at fullback. This benefits the three players and, ultimately, the entire team.

T I M E O U T
- Important Tactical Factors to Consider within The Art of Maneuvering:

- As a coach or player, always remain flexible and willing to move when opportunities occur, such as your opponent's being tired, confused, or vulnerable.

- Be aware that your rivals may create fake opportunities as traps to get you to move in the wrong direction.

- Never forget that there are multiple ways to move, directly or indirectly. Also, small groups can maneuver faster in many situations than large groups.

- Your maneuvering needs to consider other intangibles, such as an opponent's strengths or weaknesses from the right, left, center, front, back, etc.

- Be disciplined in your maneuvering but allow for creativity and feedback.

Suggested Continuous Improvement Process or Tool

An outstanding process to help you to obtain quickly and sort similar groupings for improvement is done through affinity diagramming. Affinity diagramming will often be the first step into other continuous improvement tools and processes since you gain inputs. See Chapter 15 to learn how you may implement affinity diagraming into your tactics and strategy.

♠ Being Transparent Supports Agility and Trust

So how transparent are you when coaching your players?

As a coach, your role is to lead in a way that allows your players to perform at their best. A big part of that is open communication.

For example, do you respectfully communicate with "Joe" and tell him that Sam is working hard and improving but is struggling a bit in his transition from offense to defense? As a result, do you need Joe to adjust his game and reposition himself defensively during this time to compensate? The coach's role is to place the right players in the correct positions at the right times. However, it is only successful if it is openly communicated within the team.

Knowing your players' strengths, weaknesses, and opponents is key to team success. Sharing what will happen when things go well is important and should be done. However, sharing what will happen when things don't go well or as planned is just as important. My question to you is how does this build trust with your players?

The answer is TRANSPARENCY.

As a coach, sharing critical information with your players is essential. Team members must clearly understand each player's strengths and weaknesses to adapt their strategies based on the play. So, being agile is vital for this to happen but it will only happen if you are transparent with your team members. It will not occur if you have another agenda that benefits you personally and not the team, school, league, or players.

When prepping for your competition, the same is just as important. Your players must clearly understand the other team and its players. What are their strengths and weaknesses? This discussion can be had on the practice field as plays are being developed or reinforced. The transparent discussion should also be communicated when your players review game films. Coaching on agile strategies that can be taken when needed can help players adjust on the field.

Transparency does NOT mean sharing everything all the time. As a coach there are times when some information needs to be held back until the right moment. You, as the coach, hold all the power. For instance, while it may not be an everyday event, you must maintain command and control should someone leave your organization and join your opponents. Furthermore, in a worst-case scenario, imagine the ramifications if you think there is an unknown security leak in your organization, and you share your entire game plan with the disgruntled player or coach.

We all know that big decisions and deals are handled behind closed doors. However, implementing a transparency policy within an organization is key to avoiding corruption and bribery.

As a coach, you can learn to be transparent by-

1) **Creating an environment that is both transparent and supportive.** Be clear on both professional and performance expectations for athletes and staff.

2) **Communicating the WHY.** Explain the reasoning behind why decisions are made.

3) **Sharing your knowledge.** A dedicated athlete will spend much time practicing perfecting a skill. Let them know the HOW and WHY behind it so it's done right the first time.

CHAPTER 8

ATHLETIC ART OF VARIATION IN TACTICS

Athletic Art of Variation in Tactics

"You can dream all you want, but those who aren't willing to take the risks are the posers who always have excuses for not achieving anything. If you're not willing to sacrifice, persevere, and commit to something, it's not going to happen."

Vince Papal,
Former NFL walk-on

Have you ever seen an athlete, coach, or player win a competition due to their elite ability to implement unpredictable and sometimes unconventional tactics?

There are periods in athletics when remaining stagnant may be beneficial for reaching your goals. Think, for example, when you may need a brief break, either mentally or physically, to recover. Or a quick strategic timeout to discuss what your opponents may be planning and how you will counter. However, be extremely careful when you go into a preventive tactical mindset since this is when your opponents are more likely to attack and you are most vulnerable.

Please think of how many wins or losses have been determined by the fact that one team refused to change their tactics and remained rigid and predictable. Yet, their opponents, in many cases with nothing to lose, are flexible and willing to take risks. Elite athletes and coaches are more than familiar with close matchups where both sides go back and forth on a scoreboard and are deadlocked. Perhaps even going into overtime periods. Yet the victorious team, in most cases, is the one that determines the outcomes by adjusting their tactics and thus increasing their probability of winning by being on the offensive versus defensive. Furthermore, imagine how many comeback games we have seen where one team dominated the entire game and decided to go into a preventive or stagnant mode. The competitor who is unwilling or unable to adjust according to their circumstances is vulnerable.

Picture this: In a pivotal scene in the movie *Invincible*, the Eagles and Giants are in a deadlock, and it appears they are both content with playing in overtime. After being stopped for a loss late in the game, the Eagles decide to play it safe and punt the ball. Everyone, from the coaches to players, to their disgruntled fans, knows that the Eagles are scared to take any tactical risks. Their priority remains to ensure their punter is protected at all costs while he kicks downfield. On the opposite side of the field, the sportscasters repeat what all the coaches and disgruntled fans also know. The Giants now have two tactical options: rush the Eagles and try to block the ball or set up for the punt return. This is where the movie becomes interesting. Vince Papale, played by Mark Walburg, notices that the Giants have become predictable and have telegraphed their decision. While on the line of scrimmage, Papale changes the Eagle's play and does the opposite of what his coach requested because he sees an opportunity to win the game. Did he make the right choice?

Changing the call of your head coach is quite risky and, in many situations, will be considered insubordination. However, at an elite level, there are protocols where the players may be able to change the coach's calls, specifically when the other team is not changing their tactics and is predictable. This is because if you do not vary your tactics, it is almost inevitable that your opponents will introduce variations on their side. This is why you see so many comebacks or last-minute wins when one team can adjust tactics faster than its opponents. Making yourself unpredictable and flexible allows you to attack your opponent's weaknesses quickly, often the difference between a win or loss.

TIMEOUT
- Important Tactical Factors to Consider within The Art of Maneuvering:

- Always build a strong defense first.

- Know when to take risks and when to be conservative.

- Practice many unpredictable attacking, defending, and counterattacking scenarios.

- Planning is still vital, but expect and prepare to change tactics quickly based on circumstances.

- During competitions, constantly monitor your opponent's strengths and weaknesses, and do not be afraid to change.

Suggested Continuous Improvement Process or Tool

PDCA is a great tool to help you follow an organized improvement method. PDCA is the short acronym for guiding you through planning, doing, checking, and acting. See Chapter 15 to learn how you may implement PDCA into your tactics and strategy.

⬥ Playing Favorites Will Destroy Trust

Do you unconsciously let your favorite players slide on team rules?

When I present my workshop on how to build trust in teams, I have a slide in my presentation that states, "Favoritism: the only ones that say it doesn't exist are the ones getting it." This is so true, right? The bottom line is that, yes, while the situations may vary, there will be a level of biased or unbiased favoritism that will take place within teams. This occurs because, ultimately, a coach must place the players, coaches, and team in a position where they are most likely to win. For example, coaches often favor skilled players and coaches who put the team first, communicate well, work hard, and produce positive results over others. Of course, the positive reason for becoming a favorite is quite long. But we are going to focus on showing favoritism outside the positive aspects.

You may let a starter continue to skirt or avoid the team guidelines with lower to no consequences compared to non-starters. This may manifest in the form of not having them participate in specific drills, giving permission to come late or leave early, or even allowing top performers to slack off during practice because they are going to start. Often, a less obvious but common level of favoritism can also be viewed when a coach only gives feedback to their most talented players rather than all players.

It is important to be aware of how you behave when interacting with your players.

So, what if a player only has talent but their actions and behaviors are detrimental to the team? To build and maintain trust, it is important as a coach, player, and team that you keep each other accountable.

One final thought on favoritism since it is often an issue based on playing time. In such situations, the coach does not have to explain everything but does need to talk with the team and share why some players may be playing and others are not. Communicating the WHY behind such decisions allows for transparency and understanding of what an individual needs to do for improvement.

As a coach, you can learn not to play favorites by-

1) Creating an environment that promotes excellence for all players and staff.

2) **Being approachable.** Let your staff and players know they can give you feedback.

3) **Communicating a team-first approach.** Highlight each player's strengths and weaknesses and how they impact on the team's success.

ATHLETIC ART OF ARMY ON THE MARCH

Athletic Art of Army Teams on The March

"There wasn't a single detail left out, not even the P decals on the helmets. They were peeled off after every game and put in a refrigerator to preserve freshness, then placed back on the night before the game"

Buzz Bissinger,
Author of Friday Night Lights – A Town, a Team, and a Dream

Have you ever seen an athlete, coach, or player win a competition due to their elite ability to establish contingencies in all situations?

The concept of this chapter revolves around your ability to continually improve by looking for the most efficient and rapid ways to move your teams into specific positions. As discussed, our intent is to not remain stagnant, so movement is necessary. But how can we move forward and reach our objectives without putting ourselves at risk? The frustrating and ambiguous answer is that it may depend on the situation. However, in the quote above, we cannot deny that elite coaches, players, and teams often have secrets they don't share. The tipping point between competitors that are considered equals is often found in small details.

Will the process of something as small as removing and reapplying decals win you a game? For many, they may answer with a resounding "no way". But think for a minute; you have two teams that may have similar uniforms or are all playing in the mud. To complicate matters, both teams have white helmets, and the only difference is the logos on one team's helmets, similar to the "P" for the Permian Panthers high school featured in Bissinger's book. Could the quarterback, for example, throw to the wrong person if the logos were applied poorly and all the helmets looked the same in the rain? It may sound a bit anal-retentive, but a team on the march needs to remain in a consistently combat-ready mode, so to speak.

Picture this: in the movie adaptation of *Friday Night Lights*; there is a scene where head coach Gary Gaines (played by Billy Bob Thornton) knows his team is assured victory. His team had played a near-perfect game and dictated where, when, and how his team moved across the field the entire night. Simply put, they were not only moving efficiently and swiftly against their opponents, but they also minimized their risks. It looks like nothing could go wrong with such a significant lead and the impossibility of the opponents being able to make up the difference with less than two minutes to go. As a result, he decides to play his backup running back and start resting his main starters. However, the backup was not engaged in the action and, when called upon, tried to enter the game without his helmet. Unprepared and unable to find his helmet, Gaines puts his starter back into the game. Unfortunately, this results in an unpredictable injury.

The movie accurately portrays what usually happens in such situations; the head coach is blamed for putting the star player back in the game. Others may have blamed the backup for his helmet failure and inability to be in the game at that juncture to protect the star player. It is debatable, but ultimately, an elite coach, player, or team will realize you cannot blame anyone, especially in this example, since injuries are often unpredictable. However, small details, especially in visual or verbal communication, often distinguish between winning and losing when you have a team on the march.

TIMEOUT
- Important Tactical Factors to Consider within The Army Team on the March:

- Prepare contingency options for variations in your weather and terrain.

- All your equipment and supplies should be thought of in advance.

- Practice in many different types of environments to simulate real scenarios.

- While speed, efficiency, and lowered risks are your goals, never forget the importance of coach, player, and team synchronization.

- During competitions, you must be open to change but keep your communication secret since your opponents will be listening.

Suggested Continuous Improvement Process or Tool

A great tool to help you avoid missing essential tasks that need completion is Checklists.

Checklists serve as reminders for your primary users and guides for your support so that you maintain quality and productivity. See Chapter 15 to learn how you may implement checklists into your tactics and strategy.

❧ Building Cohesiveness Leads to Trust

Do your athletes feel like they are part of a team?

Building cohesiveness in a team is crucial in creating a high-performing team. The focus should be on the individual players' strengths and how they support the team as a whole. Should uniting a team be intentional? Absolutely! A coach should always think about sharing common goals, experiences, and unity.

So, what happens when a coach doesn't focus on the team but rather on the individual player? Players will fight with one another, thus creating a divisive team. The "star" player will receive all the attention resulting in jealousy from the other teammates. Feelings of jealousy may lead to players not wanting to support the "star" player when needed on the field. Additionally, a coach may be too easy on the "liked" players and not enforce the team rules. For example, a player gets kicked off the football team because he violates University rules and gets caught cheating. The Athletic Director talks to the professor, and miraculously, this player is back on the team for the next big game. The coach's actions let the other teammates know that they can be disrespectful in school with zero consequences. The bottom line is that when a coach points out the differences between the individual players in a way that isn't supportive but instead is somewhat divisive, you will not have a cohesive team.

Social media can also influence whether a team is cohesive or not. For instance, a reporter may only pull aside a "star" player rather than several team members to interview. Whether media is in the forms of print, television, or audio, the interview or message can be biased and slanted in one direction. Social media and media, in general, are not going away. It is up to the coaches to learn how to use media to their advantage by promoting teamwork and the team. We all have our favorite teams and players. However, as a coach showing commitment to the team and players shows the importance of unity and leads to trust.

Mike Edgar wrote in *Sports Psychology Today* tips on how a coach can create a team environment and build credibility.

As a coach, you can learn to build team cohesiveness by-

1) **Encouraging open lines of communication with the team and among the players.** Open communication can be accomplished by promoting mutual respect and sharing athlete responsibilities and game strategy.

2) **Ensure that all players know their role on the team.** The coach can host team meetings where roles are defined, and players can share with their teammates what they need to be successful.

3) **Develop a shared team mission.** When players understand the goals and how they fit into achieving them, they feel a sense of ownership.

https://www.sportpsychologytoday.com/youth-sports-psychology/building-team-cohesion-for-success/

CHAPTER 10

ATHLETIC ART OF TERRAIN

Athletic Art of Terrain

*❝When I'm unstoppable, I don't need easy,
I just need possible.❞*

Bethany Hamilton,
Legendary Motivational Surfer

Have you ever seen an athlete, coach, or player win a competition due to their elite ability to adapt mentally and physically based on changing terrains?

Have you ever seen a player, coach, or team adjust their tactics or strategies based on terrain?

To answer the following question, let's brainstorm the many options available. Or, to make it easier, watch the highlights each night on a major sports channel. Without naming every sport or terrain, you will quickly see examples of rivals competing on natural surfaces such as grass, dirt, wood, clay, ice, snow, water, or sand. In addition, there are many artificial substitutes, such as synthetic surfaces. While these examples are not an exhaustive list of every terrain, you can already imagine how the environment may be a difference maker in athletics.

To complicate matters, what about other factors? For example, rain, sleet, snow, temperatures, winds, and even sunlight can alter your terrain. This is in addition to the normal wear and tear that may occur during competition. As a result, you may see equipment, or various forms of technology being used for the changes in terrain.

The most effective competitors not only expect the landscape to change but also have developed an uncanny ability to adapt to any scenario and be successful. They ultimately know when to attack or defend based on their or an opponent's strengths and weaknesses.

Picture this: in *Soul Surfer*, Bethany Hamilton (played by Anna Sofia Robb) competes on the most significant and least predictable terrain: water. To complicate matters, as the time of the championship is ending, she has only 30 seconds to catch a wave and win. However, there is a total lull in the water, and it appears as if everyone except Bethany believes she can still be victorious. While the movie shows her feeling the water with her hand, we also realize that by looking at her face, she senses her terrain is about to change and become a strength. Without giving away the ending, she can feel a massive wave developing and adjust her tactics and strategy immediately, shocking all onlookers. Oh, did we also fail to mention that beyond the unpredictability of her terrain, she is also doing this with one arm? So, we had a competitor with time, terrain, and balance against her, but also the psychological barrier of previously losing her arm to a shark.

Without a doubt, this may be an extreme example of how a competitor can adjust their tactics and strategy to their terrain. But what may have been missed by many viewers in the movie is that Bethany prepared for that moment well before the wave was formed. For example, she knew her terrain was always subject to change, so you see her doing a massive amount of cardio, weight, speed, and agility training before the competition. This leads to the differentiator between good and elite coaches, athletes, and teams: their preparation. While they may not share all their secrets, elite competitors will simulate and practice in every condition possible in preparation for the unpredictable.

TIMEOUT
- Important Tactical Factors to Consider within the Athletic Art of Terrain:

- Scout your terrain in advance, monitor, and be prepared to change your strategies and tactics as required.

- Know your strengths and weaknesses on various terrains.

- Know if your opponents are reluctant to attack or defend on various terrains.

- Understand the many intangibles of terrain, such as how it may affect communication.

- Winning should always be your top priority, but in some terrains, survival during a specific period is vital to your survival.

Suggested Continuous Improvement Process or Tool

A great process that will allow you to get immediate feedback after a competition is Retrospectives. Retrospectives should not be prolonged too long after competition since your lessons learned may be lost if feedback is delayed. See Chapter 15 to learn how you may implement retrospectives into your tactics and strategy.

◆ Trust In Yourself to Recognize and Adapt

How do you handle adversity?

As an athlete and coach, the terrain we play on doesn't always remain constant. For instance, one minute, a player could be on the football field on a warm, sunny day, and after kickoff, it could snow. What's the impact of the change in weather on the terrain and, ultimately, the game? Simply put, there is probably much more slipping and sliding on the football field. So, how do you overcome this obstacle?

Many of the decisions we make daily are subconscious habits. A basketball player knows how to dribble a ball down the court because it has been done millions of times. What requires more thought into how the ball gets dribbled down the court depends on the opposing team member's dexterity, skill, and speed. The tried-and-true method may not work with this player. Thinking outside the box and being creative by passing the ball to an unsuspecting teammate may be a strategy, or it may not.

Researchers Parker and Walsh (2017) found that mental pressure significantly impacts an athlete's performance. The strain or stress from being in competitive situations may be caused by psychological impact errors, negative feedback, and sustaining attention in a dynamic environment. All these stressors and more can play a role in the success or failure in how an athlete makes a decision on the field.

The article in *Progress in Brain Research* studied athletes assessed in high and low mental pressure conditions as well as uncertainty and fast reactive responses when making a decision. The athletes in the high-mental-pressure group delivered slower responses and reaction times compared to the low-mental-pressure group. The athletes experienced increased levels of anxiety and negative thoughts when their working memory was overwhelmed, resulting in less accurate decisions because resources were not considered. More interesting was the finding there was no difference between girl athletes and boy athletes when uncertainty was a factor. However, boy athletes were found to be more risk takers than girls when making a decision.

It is also important to recognize how feedback is given to an athlete. When coaches give negative feedback to players, they experience more anxiety-related thoughts, which negatively impact their working memory to make good decisions. The inability to make good decisions on the field can have serious consequences in a game.

To feel confident in your players and trust in their skill and decision-making in the huddle or on the field, it's important to build upon it during every practice.

As a coach, you can learn to break down impediments and solve problems by-

1) **Reducing the mental pressure on your athletes.** Lowering mental pressure can be accomplished by communicating positive, constructive feedback rather than negative feedback. Athletes will then focus their decisions and behaviors on what needs changing rather than worrying about what they did wrong.

2) **Limit distractions before a game.**

3) **Look for patterns in the opposing team.** Athletes and coaches can look for the behavioral cues displayed by their opponents. *The Innerdrive Blog* shared a great example of how Andre Agassi recognized that his opponent, Boris

Becker, would stick his tongue out to the side when he would serve the tennis ball. Agassi could then make an informed decision on what direction the tennis ball would be heading, allowing him to respond appropriately. Agassi saw the pattern and took advantage of it.

https://blog.innerdrive.co.uk/sports/decision-making-in-sport

https://www.sciencedirect.com/science/article/abs/pii/S0079612317301127

ATHLETIC ART OF THE 9 SITUATIONS

"He was a powerful, quick puncher, but his slowness of foot and his reluctance to use his left hand made him incomplete."

Jeremy Schaap,
Author of Cinderella Man, describing James Braddock

Have you ever seen an athlete, coach, or player win a competition due to their elite ability to understand situational awareness?

Have you ever known a great athlete, coach, or team who ultimately failed to reach their potential by failing to be adaptable or coachable?

As we enter chapter 11, one of the fascinating conundrums is whether all nine situations are still relevant today. For the sake of time, we will not compare all the similarities between the past and present. This is an introductory book; an entire separate manuscript could be written on the nine situations. So, we will only focus on a few key ones to start. But if you eventually examine each of these scenarios presented in *The Art of War*, you will have to answer with an overwhelming response of YES.

For example, this includes but is not limited to topics we have already presented, such as causing chaos, attacking, defending, and tricking your opponents by setting traps, which have already been discussed. While the chapter focuses on nine ground variations, we should look at our sports and how we adapt. Every sport is dynamic and in a constant state of change. This is why some athletes, coaches, and teams are in a continuous state of improvement while others, as we mentioned above, fail to reach their full potential.

Picture this: In the movie *Cinderella Man*, the James mentioned above J. Braddock (played by Russell Crow), is on an improbable winning streak and in a position possibly earn a chance to box Max Baer for the world championship, As accurately described by the author of the book, Braddock had been an incomplete boxer previously. However, in this montage of multiple fights before the championship fight, we start to see Braddock in a constant state of self-improvement. Yes, he still had the power in his punches and the quickness in each contest. However, as he progresses from one match to the next, his feet move faster, and he becomes dangerous with both hands.

At the end of the montage, without any words being spoken, you see Braddock and his trainer look into each other's eyes and nod to each other that they are now ready for Max Baer. It could be argued that Braddock was prepared because he had known and experienced all nine situations. However, to keep it simple, remember three important ones that apply to every sport. Knowing when to attack, hold your ground, or sometimes even retreat will give you a significant tactical and strategic advantage over your opponents. James J. Braddock is just one of many examples of a competitor who could adapt no matter the situation and reach his potential. Furthermore, Braddock could also be described as coachable.

T I M E O U T

- Important Tactical Factors to Consider within the 9 Situations:

- Know your opponents and your grounds in advance.

- Never rile up or motivate your opponents, especially on their grounds.

- Avoid being baited into traps when on unfamiliar grounds.

- Unpredictability, creating disruptions, or causing chaos are effective methods of gaining advantages at home or away.

- Put your opponents on the ground and into positions where they cannot escape.

Suggested Continuous Improvement Process or Tool

An outstanding process to help obtain feedback and ideas for improvement can be obtained through interviews. Interviews can be done with expected closed responses, but it is suggested that open-ended and non-judgmental questions are utilized to increase participation and improve honesty. See Chapter 15 to learn how you may implement interviewing into your tactics and strategy.

☙ Encouraging Continual Learning Builds Trust

How do you educate and train your players?

Topics such as injury prevention, nutrition, mindset or goal setting are areas in which athletes should be knowledgeable. Learning the nitty gritty skills that impact performance are essential as well. However, some athletes think they know it all. Consequently, these athletes do not acknowledge that they do NOT know everything. These athletes are a pain in your side! It is exhausting when the athletes argue and refuse to run the drills correctly.

In an article in *The Sports Journal, A Coaches Responsibility: Learning How To Prepare Athletes For Peak Performance*, Scott Johnson and his colleagues wrote that many athletes specialize in a sport at an early age. Additionally, many athletes play several sports year-round making it challenging for their mind and body to recover from the difficulties of competition.

Scott Johnson and his colleagues suggest that the nature of the coach's job is determined by the athlete's stage of development. Based on where the athlete is in their development, the coach will determine what education and skills are needed. The challenge that exists is whether the player is open to new ideas. When a coach communicates helpfully and authentically in a way that encourages learning, the athlete is much more open to accepting the guidance. This mutual player-coach relationship creates a bond of trust. The coach can support the level of trust by tailoring books, sports games, and digital magazines highlighting a skill or knowledge gap.

It is important for the coach to be a life-long learner in their sport to be effective in training athletes for peak performance. The coach must 'walk the walk' to develop trust among their players, or it will be a challenge.

Bill Beswick, a world-renowned sports psychologist, once said that a coach's job is to take the athletes to a place they have never been and likely would never get there on their own. To do that, the coach must be demanding, consistently challenging, stretching their athletes, and have high standards and expectations. The only way an athlete will meet expectations is if they possess the knowledge and skills to be successful. Of course, motivation plays a role in success, but that is a topic for another chapter.

As a coach, you can create a learning environment by:

1) **Encouraging inquiry.** Encourage players to ask questions when unsure of a play or skill.

2) **Implementing an athlete mentoring program.** Athletes with more experience and knowledge can be matched with less skilled ones.

3) **Provide real-time video analysis.** Pulling aside the player and providing immediate performance feedback is much more effective than waiting until later.

https://thesportjournal.org/article/a-coachs-responsibility-learning-how -to-prepare-athletes-for-peak-performance/

CHAPTER 12

ATHLETIC ART OF ATTACK BY FIRE

"Rudy attacks everything in his life, every conversation, every meeting, every business deal, with the same fire that he attacked me in practice every day,"

Gerry DiNardo,
Former NCAA DIV 1 coach and teammate of Rudy Ruettiger

Have you ever seen an athlete, coach, or player win a competition due to their elite ability to implement concepts that mimic the positive or negative traits of fire?

Have you ever seen an athlete, coach, or team that may not be the most skilled, yet their focus and intensity are so powerful that they ignite and motivate others to perform at a higher level?

Upon first analysis, we may believe there is nothing remotely connected to the use of fire described in *The Art of War* and athletics. However, elite coaches, players, and teams will quickly prove you wrong by telling you their strategy and tactics. Think, for example, of all the adjectives we may hear related to sports and, in many cases, are associated with a win or loss.

Think of how effective it may be to have a "red-hot" offense that "scorches" the opponent's defense. The difference between two quick teams may be "blazing" speed. You may want to "burn," "scorch," or cause your opponent's plans to go up "in flames." While these are just a few examples of fire being used as an offensive perspective, you must also understand that the opposition is trying the same strategies and tactics against you. In this case, you may want to "cool" them down when they are considered "hot." Perhaps even prevent a fire and or "extinguish" it immediately.

Picture this: Early in the movie *Rudy*, we see the title character, Rudy Ruettiger (played by Sean Astin), trying out for the Notre Dame football team. Before they start the tryouts, a coach says they have 95 scholarship players on the team yet can only dress out 60 players for home games. As a result, 35 players deemed significant enough to be awarded money to play at the school will be watching from the sidelines. He then explains to the other group of 15 potential walk-on players (including Rudy) that his job is to beat them senseless over five days and that one or two may be able to be picked for the scout team. He continues in a brutal but honest view, explaining that if they make the scout team, they will only be used to run the opponent's plays, and their best value is that they don't care if they get hurt.

So, with the odds of any of the walk-ons making the team, how could this be related to the use of fire? Using fire as a strategic and tactical concept is revealed as we watch Rudy endure the brutal tryouts. Rudy is physically overmatched for making the team, as he is brutally beaten in every football drill of the tryout process. At one point, he is so overmatched that another coach physically grabs him and tries to pull him out of an exercise, to which we see Rudy rebel telling him he can do it and jump back into the fray. Shortly after this event, the two assistant coaches present their cases to the head coach regarding whether to cut all the walk-ons.

One assistant coach adamantly makes a case for adding Rudy, while the other assistant coach dismisses him completely and states he has no athletic skills. Ultimately, the coach who argued in Rudy's defense and agreed to take him on the group of positional players he was coaching wins the argument, which will later be an excellent decision. In retrospect, we will see that Rudy was added to the team because he had an intangible that all successful coaches, players, and teams desire and respect: a teammate with an inner "fire" in their eyes and hearts, which has often proved to be more effective than skilled players who lack "fire."

TIMEOUT
- Important Tactical Factors to Consider when Discussing Fire:

- Remember to not only use fire as an adjective and establish key performance indicators to measure.

- Allow creativity when implementing a process of attack or defense, but never be haphazard.

- Remember that speed is one of the leading tactical concepts of how fast fire may accelerate or must be slowed down or suppressed during competition.

- Practice situations where you may face a competitor with an advantage of fire, or it is their weakness.

- Always seek to be the coach, player, or team that can never be accused of lacking intensity, or the internal fire needed to win. Furthermore, do not fear adding or cutting those who fit into your strategy.

Suggested Continuous Improvement Process or Tool

An outstanding process to maximize and guide you through larger team projects and goals is DMAIC. DMAIC is a much more detailed process than PDCA since it incorporates design, measurement, analysis, improvement, and control. See Chapter 15 to learn how you may implement DMAIC into your tactics and strategy.

❧ How Predictability Leads to Increased Trust

Does your team know how you will respond, regardless of the situation?

Whether you are coaching soccer, football, baseball, basketball, hockey, or any other sport, the ability for your players to predict how you will react or behave in any given situation is necessary to build their trust. The lack of knowing whether one minute you will respond by yelling, screaming, name-calling, berating a teammate, walking off the field, or calling the player over to coach on what went wrong and the tactic that should have been used. I call this a 'Jekyll and Hyde' person because you never know how they will respond.

When a player is unsure how a coach will react to a missed play or being late to practice, he will not put himself out there to be the target or coach's punching bag. The emotional fear holds your players back from learning and growing as an athlete. The need to be incognito and not stand out is a loss for the coach and team. As a coach, the focus should be on learning how to control emotions so that behaviors are consistent in any given situation. If this is a challenge for you, I will share some strategies toward the end of the chapter so you can become more 'predictable' in your behavioral responses.

Self-awareness and examining your actions as situations arise can provide consistency or lack of consistency in your reactions. Defining what 'predictability' means for you can give you a direction to work towards, as it may vary based upon the eyes of your assistant coaches, players, and administration. Once defined, you can practice physical and mental scenarios to forecast results.

Bo Hansen, 4X Australian Olympian and 3X medal winner in rowing, states that when a coach behaves predictably, the athlete feels they have a much better understanding of their coach. The athlete also knows where they stand with the coach and how to address situations. Likewise, when an athlete exhibits predictability, the coach can trust that the athlete will do as instructed. Trust is the foundation of the coach-athlete relationship.

In my book, *Magnetic Trust*, I write about the 'Predictable Rule.' The importance of being predictable is one of the most important characteristics and, unfortunately, the most overlooked. As a coach, being predictable means how you communicate and behave. Never let a member of your team question whether this is your psycho day.

As a coach, you can learn to be predictable by:

1) **Treat each person and situation consistently.**

2) **Set clear expectations.** Ensure your team understands what you want from them.

3) **Keep the same demeanor when someone comes with a situation.** Turn off what is in your head and focus on them exclusively.

https://www.athleteassessments.com/behavioral-predictability-for-building-trust-in-sport/

CHAPTER 13

ATHLETIC ART OF THE USE OF SPIES

"Ken Mile's driving style quickly adapted to the enormous power of those divine Ford engines. As an engineer and a driver, he was constantly in search of a better and lighter combination."

Author Phil Henny
describing Legendary Ford Racing Driver Ken Miles

Have you ever seen a player, coach, or team gain a strategic or tactical advantage because their opponents failed to protect their game plans?

Elite coaches, players, and teams understand the importance of consistently scouting their opponents. Not knowing the strengths or weaknesses of your opponents will guarantee a win. However, the more knowledge and intelligence you have on your opponents is often the tipping point between a loss or victory. You should always know your competition's strategies and tactics and who, what, when, where, and how they intend to win. In modern times, many scouting reports and forecasting are based on knowledge gained from analytics. However, it is crucial that obtaining intel on your rivals should always include your eyes and not just rely on statistics. So, it should always be remembered that watching films or seeing your opponents in action is vital before you compete.

Your primary focus in scouting is accurately forecasting how, when, and where your opponent plans to beat you by performing ethical intelligence gathering. Ultimately, scouting can provide unlimited data that will help you prepare and practice in advance. This data may allow you to plan to attack, defend, or counterattack properly. However, remember that you must consider the human factor beyond your advanced knowledge of strategies and tactics.

Picture this: Early in the movie *Ford Vs. Ferrari*, we see the title character, Carroll Shelby (played by Matt Damon), in an awkward situation where he is primarily in a consultant role for the Ford racing team but is being held mainly responsible for a recent Ford loss. After this loss, he is called into Ford corporate headquarters to explain why everyone on the team, including Shelby, should not be fired by Ford's president, Henry Ford II. Henry Ford is livid after the loss and contemplates scrapping the entire group based on their inability to catch and eventually beat Ferrari.

Shelby calmly yet directly tells Ford a brief synopsis of what he has scouted. First, while he was in the waiting room, he said the folder to be sent directly to Ford passed through four hands in the waiting room. Furthermore, in all likelihood, it also passed through another 20+ hands before it reached Ford's desk. This shows that Shelby was scouting his rival's plans and processes and his team's strengths and weaknesses and has identified internal waste. This waste (called Muda in process improvement terms) is unnecessary work without adding value. The goal is to eliminate wastefulness, "Muda," to speed things up.

Despite the bureaucratic wastefulness slowing down the progress that must be streamlined within their team, Shelby also tells Ford that his intel shows that they have Ferrari exactly where they need it to win. Shelby starts with specific mechanical issues, such as the car's ability to corner well, parts overheating, lack of traction, miscellaneous parts breaking, and brake problems. Yet he explains that beyond all these issues, they still turned out to be one of the fastest laps ever on the course, and Ferrari is now aware that Ford has bypassed them with speed. But the biggest shocker he tells Ford is that they have the wrong driver.

While he does not immediately reveal the driver's name (Shelby knew it was Ken Miles), he wins Ford's respect. As a result, Ford cuts all the middle people between him and Shelby, so he now reports directly to him and no one else. This is a crucial step to winning because Shelby's scouting ability to quickly identify the strengths and weaknesses of his team and his rivals was only valuable if he got support from Ford, who, in this case, represents a head coach. Furthermore, as revealed during the movie, it was vital to get Ken Miles as their driver (again, an example of Shelby scouting), and only Ford could make this happen. This means that scouting is essential but can only be helpful if implemented or supported by leadership.

TIMEOUT
- Important Tactical Factors to Consider when Discussing Scouting:

- Don't talk or brag about your sources of information; keep things quiet to ensure it continues to flow. Remember to protect your plans and not talk or show anything to rival eyes.

- Vigorously scout your opponents and remain ethical.

- Protect yourself from unethical breaches and occasionally release or display misinformation to confuse.

- Beyond being aware of outside scouts, pay attention to disgruntled team members or those with large egos who may talk too much.

- Be aware that misinformation may be feeding into your scouting process.

Suggested Continuous Improvement Process or Tool

A great tool to identify the exact reason for either success or failure is through root cause analysis and the 5 Whys. Using The 5 Whys, you can avoid accepting surface-level answers that may be missing the real cause of an issue. See Chapter 15 to learn how you may implement The 5 Whys into your tactics and strategy.

✒ Exhibiting Ethics In Scouting Builds Trust

Are you aware that your athletes, coaches, administrators, and rivals are watching what you do and listening to what you say every day?

Despite this, you may be tempted to justify ignoring, bending, or breaking internal or external rules and regulations to get a strategic or tactical advantage over your opponents by any means necessary. Regarding spying versus scouting, we have recently witnessed many examples at the pro and collegiate levels where one or more individuals have decided that the risk of not following the scouting rules was a lower risk versus a high reward for winning. The unethical use of spying rather than taking the time and energy to gather intelligence through scouting data may seem easier, but it has serious consequences.

A simple internet search will show us that many professional and collegiate leagues have had to issue various punishments to those found guilty of violating league "spying" rules on their opponents. This includes but is not limited to high-profile teams such as the Michigan Wolverines, Houston Astros, and New England Patriots, who were found guilty by their respective leagues of stealing opponents' signs. Each team had varying degrees of punishment based on their actions. There have also been many allegations that they were not the only teams who spied on their opponents; they were just the ones who were caught. Regardless of the sign-stealing debates, one more obvious and current example of blatant spying versus scouting occurred when a former St. Louis Cardinals executive was found guilty and sentenced to jail for hacking into another team scouting database. This desire to win was so great it violated the rules of sports and led to jail time, not to mention unethical.

How do we handle what may be considered spying versus scouting and install a code of ethics for all so that trust becomes the norm toward each other and protects our teams?

The first step is to NEVER allow someone within your control to violate and look the other way. As a coach or administrator, you are complicit if you tolerate ethics violations. The lack of accountability hurts the players, team, school, and league.

A recent article in *Case IQ* shares why ethics in sports should be an organization's top priority. Not only do ethics violations damage a sports organization, but they also negatively impact the careers of the victims and violators. Damages to the organization or perpetrators could result in lawsuits, fines, loss of funding and reputations. Ultimately, is lying, cheating, or stealing worth it?

Markkula Center for Applied Ethics in Santa Clara University suggests there are four key virtues in sports ethics:

1. **Fairness-** Being consistent in following rules and not allowing discrimination or advantages to influence decisions.

2. **Integrity-** Not allowing your actions to sacrifice the quality of the game.

3. **Responsibility-** Owning up to mistakes and following the rules of the game, including not allowing emotions to take over.

4. **Respect-** Treating all members of the team with honor and care which includes staff, players, officials, and fans.

It is never fun to address unethical behavior, regardless of who it is. It is easy to 'spin' the truth, so the infraction 'looks' less severe. However, most people see right through it. This is especially true when unethical occurrences are pervasive within a specific team or individual(s). Taking preventative measures by addressing policies and holding violators accountable will reduce unethical behaviors.

As a coach, you can learn to exhibit ethics by-

1) Responding to every incident immediately and reporting to the proper channels.

2) Taking every complaint seriously.

3) Protecting the whistleblower.

4) Keeping consistent and clear documentation.

5) Incorporating a Code of Conduct and Code of Ethics within the organization.

https://www.caseiq.com/resources/why-ethics-in-sports-should-be-your-organizations-top-priority/

CHAPTER 14:

EXTRA POINTS

"Success is not forever, and failure is not fatal."

NFL Hall of Fame Coach
Don Shula's Favorite Saying

Have you ever witnessed an elite group of professional players and coaches reach perfection?

If you follow athletics closely, you may have seen multiple high school or collegiate teams reach this rare level of success—an undefeated regular season, perfection in the playoffs, and, ultimately, a state or national championship game. However, on a professional level, this is an infrequent event.

Reaching the proverbial "Perfect Season" is so rare at a professional level; there is a reason why, each year, only one team is often discussed: almost 50 years since it played in the NFL. It is still the only team that has achieved this level of greatness in over 100 years of the league's existence. This team would be, of course, the 1972 Miami Dolphins, led by Coach Don Shula, who is considered by many to be one of the best strategists and tacticians in sports.

Many forms of media describe how his legendary undefeated team won every game against overwhelming odds. However, many commentators have missed how well he followed lessons

83

learned within *The Art of War* and applied them to sports. Based on the lessons learned in our manuscript, let's quickly analyze our previous 13 chapters and see how he and his team achieved athletic greatness. Not every point presented will be discussed, but it will help you know how *The Art of War* may improve your continuous improvement.

Examples of Lessons Learned:

Chapter 1 Athletic Art of Laying Plans

Movie Example: Herb Brooks showed us what is possible when an elite leader and athlete(s) understand the importance of planning to win in advance. Unbelievable feats can be accomplished when the end state is thought of first, and everything is done in preparation for the goal, which should be winning.

Actual Life Case Study: While the 1971 Miami Dolphins lost in their Super Bowl appearance, they won the next two. The 1972 team stands out since it remains the only NFL team with a perfect season. All of this began with Coach Don Shula and his players preparing to win in advance by planning around their strengths, weaknesses, opportunities, and threats.

Chapter 2 Athletic Art of Waging War Competition

Movie Example: Herman Boone showed us the importance of having a plan by also understanding all plans are useless if they cannot be executed. While many may have panicked when their starting QB was sidelined, his ability to adapt and replace his leader with a capable, if not better, teammate allows his team to win during adversity. Furthermore, Boone was able to unite his team and gain buy-in to the change of plans.

Actual Life Case Study: Don Shula and the Dolphins lost their starting QB for most of their undefeated season however he planned and adapted with a backup QB for a lengthy period while his star recovered. Furthermore, Shula's team was so united that there was no issue when the starter was inserted back into his starting role, and the backup was relegated to holding the proverbial clipboard.

Chapter 3 Athletic Art of Attack by Stratagem

Movie Example: Billy Beane showed us that in many cases, your supporting staff needs to be involved in strategic decisions, yet there can also be one leader for final decisions. For example, when he did not have the support of his scouting department, it led to changes in his staff to support a modern perspective of how strategically the Athletics were to compete with the larger market teams.

Actual Life Case Study: Don Shula surrounded himself with capable assistant coaches. While none of them may be seen as "yes men" to the Head Coach, they all did understand their commander's intent, which was what the Dolphins would need to win based on strategy and not only athletic talent.

Chapter 4 Athletic Art of Tactical Dispositions

Movie Example: Norman Dale showed us that despite his knowledge from the bench, he ultimately needed to depend on his players, who were on the front line, to be involved in tactical decisions.

Real-Life Case Study: Don Shula was famous for being a strict taskmaster and being flexible in his game plans to change his tactics based on his player's feedback. His captains, for example, could provide feedback to their coach without fear of facing an egotistical leader who felt he always knew more than his players.

Chapter 5 Athletic Art of Energy

Movie Example: Jack Lengyel gave a great example of how a team may follow their leader. If the coach lacks energy, is out of sync with his team's emotions, and cannot motivate, the team will often follow accordingly. Lackadaisical teams often mirror lackadaisical leaders.

Actual Life Case Study: Pull up any old clip of Don Shula, and you will see that he epitomized the look and the production of a leader who understood energy. He expected his staff and players to exhibit the same commitment to positive energy, which builds momentum and, as a result, a victory over teams who need help understanding energy concepts.

Chapter 6 Athletic Art of Weak and Strong Points

Movie Example: Brian Clough showed us that even when your team may be considered an underdog, the gaps in skills can be overcome with advanced knowledge of strong and weak points. Even the most dominant teams have weaknesses, and those who believe they don't are often surprised when other coaches or athletes expose them during competition.

Actual Life Case Study: As a follow-up to chapter one in the planning section, Shula and his teams often knew the strengths and weaknesses of their opponents and themselves. However, their ability to understand their opponents took their teams to elite status. They often feint weaknesses to throw their opponents off and catch them off guard. Shula was famous for quickly making game changes if his intel may have been off.

Chapter 7 Athletic Art of Maneuvering

Movie Example: George Halas showed us the importance of building flexibility within your team's maneuverability. Instead of having two players with very different skill sets who would need to share playing time, he maneuvered his lineup to place both on the field simultaneously.

Actual Life Case Study: Shula faced a similar situation to Hallas; however, he took maneuvering to a different level since he had three players who needed playing time and, again, different skill sets. For the Dolphins, he decided to rotate the three players based on their skills according to the situation. Shula may not have invented situational substitutions, but again, they may have been perfected with his team.

Chapter 8 Athletic Art of Variation in Tactics

Movie Example: Vince Papale demonstrated that with the trust of his coach, it is essential to remain flexible and take tactical risks within reason. Meaning, when he saw an opponent that could not, would not, or was just unable to stay flexible, they remained vulnerable. Teams that can surprise their opponents understand the value of variation.

Actual Life Case Study: Shula and his team understood the concept of the commander's intent. This means he had leaders on both sides of the game (offense and defense) who were empowered to change their tactics should an opportunity arise. Shula and his coaches understood the end state, meaning the commander's intent was to win the games. But they also understood they needed players to take a leadership role and make tactical adjustments in real-time to surprise their opponents by being empowered to vary tactics based on opportunities.

Chapter 9 Athletic Art of Army on The March

Movie Example: Gary Gaines demonstrated in Friday Night Lights that whenever you are operating as a team, and there is any form of movement, even the most minor details are essential. Championship teams also understand that the proverbial saying that we are often only as strong as our weakest link applies to keeping your team on track. Even the most minor distractions or unnecessary waste of time or effort will slow you down.

Actual Life Case Study: In retrospect, Shula and his team had many distractions during the season. However, they understood that many controllable and uncontrollable distractions are on a team during the season, preseason, and off-season. He had many players who may have been pushing the limits of his notorious persona of being a strict disciplinarian. Yet, the head coach, his staff, and players also knew that discipline on their march to a perfect season and Super Bowl started with reducing any wasted physical or mental obstacles.

Chapter 10 Athletic Art of Terrain

Movie Example: Bethany Hamilton provides a great example of adjusting to unpredictable terrain as she competed and practiced in advance. She was likely not only surfing on days that might have been considered easier than others. She was not looking for an easy practice session; she wanted practices and environments to mimic potential challenges.

Actual Life Case Study: The weather in Miami was and still is notoriously tricky for opponents. Between the sun, heat, and intense rainstorms in Florida, Shula and his teams were always prepared because they practiced in adverse situations. Simply put they understood their terrain and the advantages and disadvantages of playing in Florida in the early parts of the season. Furthermore,

Shula had a roster full of coaches and players who also had experience and knowledge on how to prepare for traveling to play teams in the cold northeast later in the season. Imagine the advantages of being ready to play as well on a perfect, wet, snowy, or muddy field.

Chapter 11 Athletic Art of the 9 Situations

Movie Example: James Braddock is an excellent example of a competitor who understood the acronym and concept of DOTS, which means that his strategy and tactics would depend on the situation. Of course, it is impossible to predict and prepare for every scenario that might occur. But it is not impossible to understand that, like Braddock and his trainer, they were often so in sync that they could communicate verbally and non-verbally to adjust.

Actual Life Case Study: Pull up video footage of Shula coaching and his players on the field during the undefeated season. You will notice similar traits; they understand situations will always change, but verbal and non-verbal communication within the team is a key advantage. Furthermore, they also understood that there is a huge advantage in some cases with no communication whatsoever, specifically with their opponents. They understood the importance of not trash-talking their opponents to prevent reversing from being in a winning position to motivating the losing team into a comeback.

Chapter 12 Athletic Art of Attack by Fire

Movie Example: Despite the well-known historical changes in the movie based on Rudy Ruettigers life, there is one fact that no one can deny, he is the type of player that understood the concept of attacking by fire. Certain coaches, teams, and players have an innate ability to overwhelm rivals with the idea of fire. In

Rudy's case, the argument may be made that he does this more in practice than in a game situation. But imagine how he can prepare the team each week.

Actual Life Case Study: Shula understood the importance of having players like Rudy on his team. Granted the NFL was at a higher level than the NCAA, but the intensity and lessons learned from fire still apply. While talent was necessary, the Dolphins comprised many players who were cast off or never considered candidates to make other teams. Yes, skill is important, but having self-motivated competitors compete intensely to win games and improve daily in practice was a solid strategic and tactical advantage that led to a perfect season.

Chapter 13 Athletic Art of The Use of Spies Scouts

Movie Example: Carroll Shelby understood that Ferrari was just as interested in what Ford may have been doing as much as Ford was interested in Ferrari. They may have been similar in more ways than either one may want to admit, since they constantly scout each other's technical strengths and weaknesses. Yet, as we have seen in the movie, one of the items that was a turning point was the addition of what was perhaps a secret weapon, which was in his selection of Ken Miles as his driver. Simply put, Shelby had already scouted a driver skilled in driving sub-optional equipment and therefore was overlooked and underestimated by Ford and Ferrari. Most importantly, he kept his intel private.

Real-Life Case Study: Shula was a purist known for his teams not only watching advanced films on his opponents but also film edits specifically focused on the Dolphins' strengths and weaknesses. It's not a new concept, but his ability to change players based on matchups and situations can be argued as a blueprint for many modern coaches. For example, scouting a team in advance is a concept introduced previously, but being able to change players based on matchups during a game could be argued as being mastered by Shula. If he saw a weakness before or, more importantly, during a game, he would adjust accordingly, and he knew his rivals' game plan or intentions perhaps better than his opponents.

CHAPTER 15

PROCESS IMPROVEMENT TOOLBOX

Continuous Improvement Processes and Tools

Both in the past and future, winning players, coaches, and teams all share one common trait. That is, to consistently win and have prolonged success, it is vital to be in a state of continuous improvement. If you are serious about beating your competition, it is vital to gain knowledge from strategic classics such as *The Art of War* and become familiar with various continuous improvement processes and tools.

Below is an introduction or review of some suggested core items to put in your proverbial continuous improvement toolbox. None of the items below will guarantee a win or even promise that you will slightly improve. But, if used correctly, they are often the foundations for achieving success and staying at the top. This is not an extensive list, rather an introduction, but it is essential to understand that they will not be used sequentially. Like any process or tool, you must beware of the DOTS theory, which is common in sports (Depends On The Situation).

However, one suggestion before you continue is that all items below may seem simple enough. Bringing in an unbiased or experienced expert for the best results is often a good idea. This is not to say that you cannot use these tools to improve yourself, only that having someone from the outside will often eliminate known or unknown biases. Furthermore, they are often experienced in coaching others in continuous improvement.

Remember that entire books and classes are often devoted to the specific topics introduced below, so it is important to research each to gain a tactical or strategic advantage.

Successful teams will often bring in unbiased trained professionals to conduct the meetings and obtain information at various levels of complexity.

Affinity Diagrams: Winners are constantly seeking as much participation from the team as possible to generate new ideas for improvement and establish buy-in. Affinity diagramming is an excellent collaborative method of gaining many ideas. A standard method for gaining inputs before you diagram similar categories is to have your individuals write their ideas for improvement on index cards or sticky notes. Sticky notes because all ideas are then organized based on their relationships. These relationships are then diagramed to represent categories a team may need to improve visually.

Benchmarking: Winners recognize that it is vital that they continuously measure and monitor their athletic performances. While it may be argued that the most crucial benchmarking method is based on wins and losses. However, to reach elite status, players, coaches, and teams closely monitor additional specific goals or targets and measure if they remain stagnnt, regressing, or improving.

Brainstorming: Winners understand that when you need to obtain many creative ideas in a short period it is hard to beat brainstorming. If you are not brainstorming and seeking new ways to improve, your competition will utilize this technique to win. In the past, it was common to conduct brainstorming sessions in person. Still, you should implement an electronic method to increase participation and avoid any fears of suggesting change. You can use the Affinity diagram above.

Checklists: Winners understand that even the most minor details can be the difference between a win and a loss. As a result, they often create checklists to minimize the risk of forgetting to complete tasks and establish a way to improve consistency and quality. This means that at some point in time, you may need someone else to fulfill the role of another, and it is essential to have a guide already in place to ensure productivity is maintained.

DMAIC: Winners will often use this Six Sigma (a method of improving processes) when quality improvement is required. Every process starts with defining what needs improvement, followed by measuring, analyzing, improving, and control.

Interviews: Winners understand vital improvement ideas are often obtained by talking directly to individuals. Especially if they are on the front lines of competition, while it is not a foolproof way of identifying and improving, asking a combination of closed or open questions, will aid in learning from verbal and nonverbal feedback.

PDCA: Winners follow a basic but important pattern of improvement through the acronym that represents four significant steps to positive development. This is planning, doing, checking, and acting. Failure to achieve success in all four areas will usually lead to defeat.

Process Mapping: Winners map out both their current and future processes. Often, talking about a process or just writing it down, needs to provide a visual representation to look for specific areas of improvement. When you have a visual map available, it is often helpful in identifying bottlenecks that may be blocking or significantly reducing your productivity.

Retrospectives: Winners understand that after a competition, it is essential to meet and discuss topics such as what went right, areas that need improvement, and what should continue. However, athletics are highly dynamic, so it is often important to conduct feedback sessions periodically before and during competitions to adjust.

Roles and Responsibilities: Winners understand while there are many similarities in sports, your roles and responsibilities must be clearly defined. One of the main frustrations that can lead to friction in sports is when there is ambiguity over accountability, which should be defined and practiced before competing.

Root Cause Analysis- 5 Whys: Winners understand that accepting the first answer to why a positive or negative event may have occurred in sports is never adequate. To discover the root cause, asking a series of whys is often necessary to identify and improve situations at their root. It would help if you found the actual cause of your success or failures to improve in the most needed areas.

Surveys: Winners understand the importance of allowing a non-judgmental method of feedback. While interviews are very effective, only some are willing to provide exactly where improvement is needed. Setting up a method of obtaining feedback for improvement without fear of retaliation or judgment will help you gain information that may not have always been shared verbally.

SWOT: Winners learn to gather and use information on strengths, weaknesses, opportunities, and threats to gain an advantage. Gaining intelligence on yourself and your competition is often a great starting point for any game plan.

*Bonus Tools:

OODA Loop: Winners understand that in athletics, those who can make wise decisions the fastest are often victorious. As important as understanding and utilizing SWOT and PDCA within your game plans, another real-time decision option is available. The OODA Loop, which means (Observe/Orient/Decide/Act) was created by a United States Air Force Colonel named John Boyd. Imagine using the same principles as a fighter jet pilot within your role as a coach or player. For a basic example, let's say your opponents are rapidly counterattacking (Observe), you need to change your positioning (Orient), you decide that their weakest player now has the ball and is prone to turnovers (Decide), and you immediately apply high pressure (Act), which leads to a turnover.

PERT: Winners understand there are times when you must forecast numbers. Statistical forecasting often scares those unsure, unwilling, or unaware of its importance. One method of determining the most likely result when working with numbers can be obtained by using a pert calculator. Which is a weighted time estimate. (Estimated Fastest Time + 4 x Estimated Most Likely Time + Estimated Slowest Time) / 6. PERT is an acronym for Program Evaluation and Review Technique.

SOURCES

Herb Brooks quotes. Herb Brooks Foundation. (n.d.). Retrieved April 26, 2023, from https://www.herbbrooksfoundation.com/herb-brook squotes

YouTube. (2017, September 10). *Herman Boone Full interview.* YouTube. Retrieved April 29, 2023, from https://www.youtube.com/watch?v =kMI8yMXXuW8

Lewis, M. M. (2011). *Moneyball: The art of winning an unfair game.* W.W. Norton.

Horner, S. (2021, March 1). *Jimmy Chitwood recalls 'Hoosiers' with Dan Patrick.* The Indianapolis Star. Retrieved April 30, 2023, from https://www.indystar.com/story/sports/2021/02/28/jimmy-chitwood-recalls-hoosiers-dan-patrick/6864110002/

YouTube. (2014, August 6). *Jack Lengyel on setting goals.* YouTube. Retrieved May 1, 2023, from https://www.youtube.com/watch?v =J22kE9IWhoE

Aaron-Flanagan, & Dave-Armitage. (2020, May 28). *Brian Clough's greatest quotes - 152 brilliant lines from iconic forest manager.* Dailystar.co.uk. Retrieved May 4, 2023, from https://www.dailystar. co.uk/sport/football/brian-clough-greatest-quotes-forest -22099030

Benson, M. (2008). *Winning words: Classic quotes from the World of Sports*. Taylor Trade Pub.

SJ Magazine. (2017, August 16). *Vince Papale tells us how to achieve your dreams*. SJ Magazine. https://sjmagazine.net/people/vince-papale-tells-us-achieve-dreams#:~:text=’%20You%20can%20dream%20all%20you,it’s%20not%20going%20to%20happen.%E2%80%9D

Bissinger, B. (2020). *Friday night lights: A Town, a team, and a dream*. Hachette Books.

I don’t need easy. Bethany Hamilton. (2022, April 25). https://bethanyhamilton.com/%E2%80%8Bi-dont-need-easy/

Schaap, J. (2005). *Cinderella Man*. Orion.

McGee, R. (n.d.). *The story of Notre Dame icon Rudy Ruettiger? it’s almost too good to be true*. ESPN. https://www.espn.com/college-football/story/_/id/28231473/the-story-notre-dame-icon-rudy-ruettiger-almost-too-good-true

Henny, P., & Shelby, C. (2004). *Just call me Carroll: Racing stories*. Editions Cotty.

Shula, D., & Blanchard, K. H. (1995). *Everyone’s a coach: You can inspire anyone to be a winner*. Harper Business.

https://online.utpb.edu/about-us/articles/communication/how-much-of-communication-is-nonverbal/

ABOUT THE AUTHORS

Dr. Heather Williamson

Specializing in performance management and organizational development, Dr. Heather Williamson heads Transformation Group, LLC. Since 2007, she has worked with a diverse array of clients in an effort to provide the highest quality executive coaching so her clients create high performing teams. Dr. Heather's areas of expertise include leadership, management development, building employee trust, time management, succession planning, strategic planning and organizational assessments.

The latest achievement of Dr. Williamson is becoming a #1 Bestselling author for her book, *Magnetic Trust: How Great Leaders Keep Top Performers and Get Extraordinary Results*.

Recently, you can find Dr. Heather giving leadership tips and strategies on her YouTube channel at Dr. Heather Williamson. She is an active public speaker and has presented lectures regarding achievement motivation, subordinate leadership satisfaction, creating high performing teams and building employee trust.

Dr. Williamson earned her Ph.D. from Virginia Commonwealth University. She holds a Master of Science in psychology and a Bachelor of Science in psychology from the same institution. Dr. Williamson has been active and held leadership roles in many associations including the Powhatan Chamber of Commerce and Executive Women International. Dr. Williamson was also an adjunct instructor for Virginia Commonwealth University's School of Business for several years. Dr. Heather has been married to her husband, Kent, for twenty-seven years and they have a seventeen-year-old son, Temple.

Coach MD Gross

Coach M.D. Gross was taught and mentored on the athletic strategies and tactical advantages found within The Art of War under the tutelage of leaders who served alongside historic masterminds such as General George S. Patton and General Mathew Ridgeway.

A seasoned innovator, Coach Gross has taught and coached thousands of varsity, collegiate, and professional athletes and coaches for over thirty years through a unique, easy-to-learn, streamlined blueprint for winning. His specialty includes combining and simplifying complex topics from The Art of War and process improvement through analyzing sports movies.

Coach Gross received his Bachelor of Science in Mass Communications from Virginia Commonwealth University and a Master of Science in Management, concentrating in leadership, from Troy University.

WORK WITH US

Want to improve your competitive knowledge and skills? Change to- Are you a coach or athlete looking to take your team or skills to the next level? With over 47 years of combined experience in both sports coaching and psychology, we are ready to help you!

Bring Coach Gross and Dr. Heather to your business or organization.

Visit **https://timeoutcoaches.weebly.com**

or give us a call at **+1 804 568 9175**

Email:

Coach Gross: **timeoutcoachgross@gmail.com**

Dr. Heather: **Timeoutcoachwilliamson@gmail.com**

IF YOU ARE SEEKING A TACTICAL AND STRATEGIC EDGE OVER YOUR COMPETITION, THIS BOOK IS FOR YOU.

Coach Gross and Dr. Williamson are creative at breaking down the complex ideas of Sun Tzu's *The Art of War*, through the use of popular sports movies. The tools and movie examples they share are entertaining and resonate with anyone who wants to improve their athletic skills and knowledge. As a coach, athlete, or team you will learn how to navigate challenges and make decisions that will lead your organization to victory.

Coach M.D. Gross was taught and mentored on the athletic strategies and tactical advantages found within *The Art of War* under the tutelage of leaders who served alongside historic masterminds such as General George S. Patton and General Mathew Ridgeway. A seasoned innovator, Coach Gross has taught and coached thousands of varsity, collegiate, and professional athletes and coaches for over thirty years through a unique, easy-to-learn, streamlined blueprint for winning. His specialty includes combining and simplifying complex topics from *The Art of War* and process improvement through analyzing sports movies.

Dr. Heather Williamson is a "Leadership Coach" and #1 Best-Selling Author. She has led Transformation Group, LLC for over seventeen years. She coaches people on how they can excel leading their team by building trust and helping them understand the role they play in the success of their organization. In addition, Dr. Heather is a national sought after speaker on leadership-related topics and an Executive Coach working with professionals in group settings and one-on-one. She lives in Powhatan, Virginia with her husband, Kent and son, Temple.